Corey Huff

Japan Travel Guide 2024 (Full Color Pocket Guide)

A Budget-Friendly Guide to City Attractions, Tours, and Must-See Events with Maps and Photos.

Table of Contents

Introduction

The first time I set foot on Japanese soil, the experience was nothing short of magical. It was a chilly spring morning when my grandfather and I disembarked from a plane at Narita Airport, a bustling gateway to a land steeped in history and tradition. We were there on a trade visit, but for me, an eager teenager at the time, it was the beginning of a lifelong adventure. My grandfather, a seasoned traveler with a penchant for uncovering the world's hidden gems, was my guide into this mesmerizing world. As we navigated through the crowded streets of Tokyo, I was enchanted by the harmonious blend of the old and the new, the serene temples amidst towering skyscrapers, and the quiet, respectful demeanor of its people. It was in these early days, walking alongside my grandfather, that I discovered the profound depth of Japan's culture, a depth that has drawn me back, time and again, over two decades.

Our initial journey took us far beyond the typical tourist trails. My grandfather, with his insatiable curiosity, led us to places that seemed untouched by time. In Kyoto, we wandered into an ancient teahouse hidden by cherry blossoms, where the art of the tea ceremony was performed with a grace and precision that seemed otherworldly. In Osaka, we ventured into the heart of the city's vibrant food scene, discovering a tiny, family-run takoyaki stall that, despite its modest appearance, served up flavors so rich and complex they haunted me for years to come. These experiences, shared with my grandfather, were my first glimpse into the real Japan, a country of immense beauty and subtlety, where every detail has meaning, and every tradition tells a story.

Over the years, my fascination with Japan has only deepened. Each visit has been an opportunity to peel back another layer of this intricate society, to learn more about its people and their way of life. I've celebrated New Year's Eve at a Shinto shrine, surrounded by thousands of locals ringing in the new year with joy and reverence. I've bathed in the healing waters of an onsen in the remote mountains of Hokkaido, where the silence was so profound it seemed to echo. I've explored the neon-lit streets of Akihabara, immersing myself in Japan's cutting-edge technology and pop culture, and I've found peace in the minimalist beauty of a Zen garden, where every stone and every raked line of sand seemed to hold a universe of meaning.

Japan, to me, is a country of contrasts and contradictions, where the past and the future coexist in a delicate balance. It's a place where the hustle and bustle of city life gives way to tranquil gardens and temples, where the frenetic energy of modernity is tempered by the timeless rituals of tradition. This duality is at the heart of Japan's charm, a reminder that in the midst of rapid change, there are elements of our humanity that remain constant, timeless.

In writing this guide, my aim is not just to share with you the sights and sounds of Japan, the must-visit destinations and hidden corners I've discovered on my journey. More than that, I hope to convey the essence of Japan, the spirit of a country that has captivated me for over two decades. Through these pages, I invite you to explore Japan not just as a tourist, but as a traveler eager to connect with the soul of a place, to experience its joys and sorrows, its quirks and serenities, as if through the eyes of someone who calls it home.

So, dear reader, pack your bags and bring your curiosity. Let us set forth on an adventure that transcends the ordinary, an exploration of Japan that goes beyond the surface to touch the very heart of what it means to journey through the Land of the Rising Sun. Welcome to Japan, a journey that, much like my first steps alongside my grandfather, promises to be nothing short of extraordinary.

Welcome to Japan

Welcome to Japan, one of my favorite countries when it comes to vacation. Over the last twenty years, I've explored every corner of this amazing place and found something new and exciting every time. Japan mixes the old and the new in ways that you have to see to believe. You can be looking at a huge, modern skyscraper one minute and find yourself in a peaceful, ancient temple the next. It's like stepping through time.

In cities like Tokyo, the energy is electric. Buildings reach up to the sky, and the streets are always buzzing. But just a short walk away, you can discover quiet spots where the world seems to slow down. Kyoto takes you even further back in time with its beautiful old houses and the elegance of geishas walking through the streets. The cherry blossoms in spring turn the city into a pink wonderland that looks like it's straight out of a painting. But Japan isn't just about its cities. The countryside offers its own quiet beauty. Mountains like those in the Japanese Alps are breathtaking, and the small villages feel like they're from another era, where life moves at a gentle pace.

Visiting Japan lets you dive into a culture that's rich and fascinating. Trying out a tea ceremony is about more than just drinking tea; it's a way to connect and appreciate the moment, showing how every meeting is special and worth cherishing. Japanese art and theater are also incredible, letting you see stories come to life in vivid colors and movements. And we can't forget about the food! Japanese food is an adventure all by itself. Whether it's the taste of fresh sushi or the fun of trying street food, every meal is a chance to try something delicious and beautifully made.

What really makes Japan stand out, though, are the people. Japanese hospitality, or *omotenashi*, means you're always treated with kindness and respect. It's in the way people go out of their way to help you if you're lost, or how chefs prepare your food with so much care. This kindness has made all my trips here unforgettable and is a big reason why I keep coming back.

Japan is a land of contrasts, where tradition meets the future. It's a place full of surprises, where you can ride super-fast trains, relax in peaceful gardens, or soak in a hot spring under the open sky. My journeys here have taught me that Japan isn't just a place you visit. It's an experience that touches all your senses and stays in your heart long after you leave.

So, to everyone coming to Japan for the first time, get ready for an adventure. A world of discovery, tradition, and warm welcomes awaits you.

Japan Map

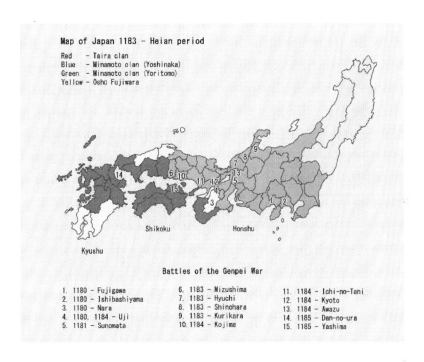

Map of Japan 1183 – Heian period

Red   – Taira clan
Blue   – Minamoto clan (Yoshinaka)
Green – Minamoto clan (Yoritomo)
Yellow – Oshū Fujiwara

Shikoku

Honshu

Kyushu

Battles of the Genpei War

1. 1180 – Fujigawa
2. 1180 – Ishibashiyama
3. 1180 – Nara
4. 1180, 1184 – Uji
5. 1181 – Sunomata

6. 1183 – Mizushima
7. 1183 – Hyuchi
8. 1183 – Shinohara
9. 1183 – Kurikara
10. 1184 – Kojima

11. 1184 – Ichi-no-Tani
12. 1184 – Kyoto
13. 1184 – Awazu
14. 1185 – Dan-no-ura
15. 1185 – Yashima

Credits: Artanisen via Wikimedia Commons

13

A Brief History of Japan

Credits: New York Public Library via Wikimedia Commons

Japan's history is as fascinating and vibrant as its cities and landscapes. This journey through time starts in the distant past and stretches all the way to the modern Heisei era, showing Japan's growth into a world leader that wields significant influence on a global scale. Japan's unique position, both geographically isolated as an island nation and yet

14

close to the vast Asian continent, has played a crucial role in its development. This blend of isolation and proximity has allowed Japan to adopt cultures and ideas from neighboring countries while cultivating its distinctive customs and practices. It's this combination of influences that has shaped the captivating country we know today.

The story begins with the Jomon period, a time stretching back to 10,000 B.C., where Japan was home to tribes and clans living off the land as hunters and gatherers. These early inhabitants crafted rope-patterned pottery, known as Jomon, marking one of the earliest forms of artistic expression found in Japan. The narrative continues with the Yayoi period around 300 B.C., when Japan saw the introduction of rice cultivation, metalworking, and the potter's wheel, thanks to influences from China and Korea. This era was named after a district in Tokyo where artifacts from this time were uncovered, showcasing a significant leap in agricultural development.

As the Yayoi culture expanded from the southern tip of Kyushu to northern Honshu, it became clear that this wasn't just a time of agricultural advancement but also a period of social and political evolution. The distinction between the earlier Jomon people and the Yayoi was notable, with the latter's culture replacing the former's hunter-gatherer lifestyle with settled farming communities. This transition set the stage for the Kofun period, which lasted until 538 A.D., characterized by the construction of massive burial mounds for clan leaders, symbolizing a unification under powerful families.

The Asuka period, beginning in 538 A.D., introduced Buddhism to Japan, marking a significant transformation in Japanese society with its artistic and socio-political changes. The Yamato clan emerged as a dominant force, influencing the southern part of Japan with principles borrowed from Chinese culture, including a new constitution and court hierarchy established by Prince Shotoku. This period was a turning point, laying the foundations for Japan's intricate relationship between its rulers and the governed, a theme that would recur throughout its history.

During the Nara period, the first permanent capital was established in Heijo-kyo, now known as Nara. This period was also marked by natural disasters and epidemics, leading to an increased emphasis on Buddhism as a means of seeking divine protection. The Heian period followed, with the capital moving to Kyoto, where it remained for over a millennium. This era saw the expansion of the Yamato court's influence and the beginning of political decline due to internal conflicts and a focus on cultural pursuits over governance.

The narrative of Japan's history is rich with periods of war and peace, from the rise of the samurai class and the establishment of the shogunate to the unification of Japan under powerful leaders like Oda Nobunaga, Toyotomi Hideyoshi, and Tokugawa Ieyasu. The Edo period brought about a time of isolation and cultural flourishing, while the

Meiji Restoration in the 19th century catapulted Japan into the modern era, emphasizing industrialization and the adoption of Western influences.

Throughout the 20th century, Japan faced significant challenges, including participation in World War II, but it emerged as an economic powerhouse in the post-war era, known for its technological innovations and robust economy. The Heisei period, starting in 1989, continued this trend of progress and modernization, despite challenges such as natural disasters and economic recessions.

Today, Japan stands as a testament to resilience and innovation, a nation proud of its heritage while leading the way in technology and global culture. From its ancient roots to its current status as a technological titan, Japan's journey through history is a story of adaptation, innovation, and the unique spirit of its people.

Understanding Japan

Exploring Japan reveals a rich mosaic of culture, etiquette, and traditions as intricate as it is profound. This journey isn't just about recognizing the surface aspects of Japan but about appreciating the deeply rooted values and practices that define this unique island nation. From the serene rituals of tea ceremonies to the lively streets of Tokyo, every aspect of Japanese life is filled with a sense of purpose and beauty.

Japanese Culture

Japanese culture is deeply rooted in a respect for harmony, order, and the natural world. This is visible in Shintoism, Japan's indigenous spirituality, which sees spirits or kami in all aspects of nature, from majestic mountains to small household objects. This reverence for nature influences everything from architecture to cuisine, ensuring actions are in harmony with the natural world.

Buddhism, introduced in the 6th century, intertwines with Shinto practices, adding philosophical depth to the Japanese worldview. Concepts like impermanence and mindfulness shape societal attitudes toward life, death, and the arts.

Japan's Etiquette

Japanese society places a strong emphasis on etiquette, a complex web of social rules designed to maintain harmony and respect. This isn't about rigid protocols but about showing consideration for others, deeply ingrained in the Japanese mindset.

The bow, a gesture of respect varying by situation and relationship, is a visible aspect of this etiquette. Language also reflects this, with varying levels of politeness encoded in speech, reflecting relationships between speakers and listeners.

Gift-giving is another art, characterized by thoughtful selection and presentation, integral to social and professional interactions. The rituals surrounding giving and receiving, from gift wrap to presentation, highlight this practice's importance.

Japan's Traditions

Japan's calendar brims with matsuri (festivals) and seasonal celebrations, showcasing rich cultural heritage. From nationwide events like cherry blossom viewing and Obon to local festivals celebrating history and spirituality, these gatherings are vibrant community expressions.

The tea ceremony, more than preparing and drinking matcha, is a meditative practice embodying harmony, respect, purity, and tranquility. Conducted in specially designed spaces, it reflects the Japanese appreciation for simplicity and the fleeting nature of moments.

Ikebana, the art of flower arranging, is a disciplined form where nature and humanity converge. It's reflective of wabi-sabi, the beauty in imperfection and simplicity.

Planning Your Trip

This essential packing list for Japan will help you prepare everything you need for a smooth trip, encouraging you to pack light and be ready for almost any situation in Japan.

Traveling with minimal luggage is always the best approach, and fortunately, you won't need to pack much to be well-prepared for your journey to Japan.

Essentials for Your Japan Journey

Organizing your trip to Japan might initially feel daunting, but breaking it down into manageable steps simplifies the process. Here are the essentials you need for your trip;

- **Passport:** Ensure it's valid for at least six months with one blank page available.
- **Visa**: Check whether you need a visa beforehand, as many countries are exempt from

this requirement for Japan. For further information, refer to our visa guide for Japan.

- **Flight Tickets**: While e-tickets are common, having a printed copy can be useful, especially for presenting to airport personnel. Use flight comparison websites to find the best deals on flights to Japan.

- **Hotel Reservations**: Printed confirmations can aid hotel staff and are handy for your reference. If possible, get the address in Japanese to assist taxi drivers. Remember, you'll need to provide the address of your accommodation when completing your landing card for immigration.

- **Japan Rail Pass**: If extensive train travel is in your plans, a Japan Rail Pass might be a wise investment. For insights and purchasing options, consult our detailed analysis.

- **Credit and Debit Cards**: VISA and MasterCard are widely accepted; American Express, less so. Inform your bank of your travel plans to avoid issues. Additionally, bring an ATM card for cash withdrawals. For tips on accessing funds, our guide covers the essentials relevant across Japan.

- **Document Copies**: Use your smartphone to photograph your passport and both sides of your credit cards, emailing the images to yourself. This ensures you have all necessary information and emergency contacts if you lose your documents.

- **Wifi and SIM Car**d: Obtaining a data-only SIM card or accessing public wifi in Japan is straightforward. Our comprehensive guides to Japan esims, physical SIM cards, and pocket wifi offer all the details you need.

- **Maps:** While digital maps are useful, a physical map provides a quick overview. Periplus produces some of the best English-language maps for Tokyo, Kyoto, and Osaka. For a country-wide map, their Japan edition is unrivaled in English.

- **Guidebook**: In addition to online resources, a physical guidebook is great for planning and reading during your flight. We recommend the

Lonely Planet Japan for country-wide travel or the Lonely Planet Kyoto City guide for focused visits to Kyoto and surrounding areas. Though I may be partial, having contributed to these guides, their value for travelers is undeniable.

Packing for Kyoto

Navigating Japan's efficient and user-friendly public transport system is a breeze, making a rolling suitcase and a daypack perfect for most urban adventures. For those planning to explore Kyoto and other cityscapes without venturing into the great outdoors overnight, this combination is ideal. Kyoto Station, among others, offers large lockers suitable for storing your suitcase temporarily after vacating your accommodation. For longer storage needs, a luggage office beneath Kyoto Station has you covered.

What to Wear in Japan

The climate in Japan varies significantly throughout the year, from sweltering summers to chilly winters.

Adhering to time-tested travel wisdom, opt for layered clothing and breathable materials. Cotton and linen are excellent choices, along with advanced, moisture-wicking fabrics from brands like UnderArmor, particularly during warmer months. These materials are a boon for underwear and are suitable for all. Less advisable is denim, due to its weight and moisture retention. Given the amount of walking you're likely to do, comfort is key.

Footwear should be light and suitable for walking. Unless you're tackling Kyoto's tougher trails, heavy-duty hiking boots aren't necessary. Many find that running shoes are adequate for lighter hikes.

A lightweight fleece jacket is surprisingly useful year-round, offering warmth in overly air-conditioned transport and venues. Additionally, a compact, quick-drying towel can be a lifesaver for extra drying needs.

Packing Toiletries for Your Trip

A comprehensive toiletry bag is essential to avoid any discomfort on your travels. In Japan, convenience stores like 7-11, Lawson, and Family Mart are everywhere, making it easy to replenish your supplies. For more specific health and pharmaceutical needs, large drugstores near train stations stock a wide variety of products, including local versions of common over-the-counter items. Communication can often be managed with patient and slow speaking when seeking assistance.

Essential items for your toiletry kit include:

- Shower essentials like body wash and shampoo.
- Tooth cleaning necessities: don't forget your toothpaste and toothbrush.
- Protective gear against the sun, including high SPF sunscreen, quality sunglasses that block

UV rays, and a hat, especially useful in the warm spring and summer months.

- Deodorant: Stick or solid forms are travel-friendly and comply with most security standards for carry-on luggage.

- Medications for stomach upset or diarrhea. While Japan's food safety standards are high, the shift to a local diet or simply indulging too much might unsettle your stomach.

- Pain relievers (Note: Check regulations for bringing medication into Japan).

- Remedies for colds and allergies, including throat lozenges and antihistamines (Note: Be aware of Japan's specific rules regarding medication importation).

- Feminine hygiene products.

- Shaving supplies, including razors and shaving cream or gel.

- A basic First Aid kit, with bandaids for minor injuries or blisters.

- A well-designed toiletry bag, preferably one that can hang on a door, helps keep your items accessible and organized.

Gearing Up with Electronics

Bringing along your smartphone is a given, so don't forget its charger and cable. Since Japan uses two-prong outlets, lacking the third grounding pin found in some other countries, packing a universal adapter is a smart move to ensure your devices stay charged. Should you leave these behind, electronic stores throughout Japan have you covered.

The same reminder goes for tablets, Kindles, or laptops: the charger is key!

Given the likelihood of using your phone for navigation and capturing memories, its battery might deplete quickly. A portable power bank can be a lifesaver, offering your phone an energy boost while you explore.

For internet access, consider purchasing a data-only SIM card once in Japan, which is a cost-effective alternative to roaming charges.

Since your smartphone might be the most valuable item you carry, protecting it with a durable case is wise. Brands like Otterbox offer sturdy cases to shield your phone from accidental drops.

Japan's picturesque scenery might inspire you to go beyond your smartphone's camera capabilities. Consider enhancing your phone with attachable lenses for zoom, wide-angle, or fisheye shots. Alternatively, investing in a compact camera from Canon could elevate your photography, capturing the beauty of Japan with greater clarity and versatility.

Best Times to Visit Japan

Discovering the ideal time to journey through Japan involves aligning your travel plans with the country's seasonal beauty and cultural events. Japan dazzles travelers with its natural and cultural tapestry, offering unique experiences across different times of the year.

Optimal Seasons for Visiting Japan

The prime seasons for exploring Japan are spring (March to May) and fall (September to November). These periods highlight Japan at its most picturesque, adorned with the soft hues of cherry blossoms or the fiery colors of autumn leaves. However, these are also peak times for tourism, meaning popular spots may be busier than usual.

Summer (June to August) is perfect for adventure enthusiasts eager to trek through the cooler mountain regions, such as the Japanese Alps and the untamed national parks of Hokkaido. In contrast, the rest of Japan experiences a hot and humid climate, with a rainy season stretching from late May through mid-July.

Winter (December to February) transforms northern Japan into a snowy wonderland, alive with festivals and cultural celebrations that light up the shorter days.

Being mindful of Japan's national holidays can enhance your visit. Shogatsu (Japanese New Year), Obon (mid-August or July, varying by region), and Golden Week (April 29 to May 5) see an influx of domestic travelers.

Japan Month-by-Month for Traveling

January: Celebrate the New Year with locals, a significant event across Japan with traditions and festivities. Visit temples, partake in Hatsumode (first shrine visit of the year), and experience the lively atmosphere.

February: Sapporo's Snow Festival showcases incredible ice and snow sculptures. It's a magical time to enjoy winter sports in regions like Hokkaido.

March: The anticipation of cherry blossoms begins, with warmer areas starting to bloom. Cultural events and preparations for sakura (cherry blossom) viewing start to take place.

April: Peak cherry blossom season across much of Japan, especially in iconic spots like Kyoto and Tokyo. Parks fill with locals and tourists enjoying hanami (flower viewing) parties.

May: Golden Week brings a series of holidays and festivals. The pleasant spring weather makes it an excellent time for sightseeing and outdoor activities.

June: The start of the rainy season brings hydrangeas into full bloom, offering beautiful scenes, particularly in temples and gardens.

July: Festivals like Kyoto's Gion Matsuri and the Tanabata Festival occur, providing insight into Japan's rich cultural traditions.

August: Obon week sees Japan honor ancestors' spirits with dances (Bon Odori), lanterns, and festivities. It's a time of vibrant cultural expression and family gatherings.

September: As temperatures cool, early autumn colors begin to show in the northern regions, and traditional autumn festivals take place.

October: The autumn foliage reaches its zenith in many parts of Japan, creating breathtaking landscapes in gardens and temples.

November: The colors of fall spread to the southern regions, offering a last chance to witness the splendid autumn hues before winter sets in.

December: End-of-year festivities and illuminations brighten up the cities, while in the north, snow begins to cover the landscapes, signaling the start of the ski season.

Japan's Climate

Japan's climate from January to December reveals a country that undergoes dramatic changes, presenting travelers with varying experiences depending on the destination and month of visit.

Tokyo: Experiences mild winters and hot, humid summers. Spring and autumn are particularly pleasant, marked by cherry blossoms and colorful leaves.

Kyoto: Known for its stunning seasonal transformations, especially the spring cherry blossoms and autumn foliage, which are celebrated with numerous festivals.

Osaka: Shares a similar climate to Kyoto and Tokyo but is slightly warmer, making outdoor activities comfortable most of the year.

Hokkaido: Offers cool summers ideal for hiking and exploring. Winters are cold, perfect for snow sports and enjoying the famous Sapporo Snow Festival.

Okinawa: Enjoys a subtropical climate, making it a year-round destination for beach-goers, with warmer temperatures even in winter.

Japanese Phrases for Travelers

One of the crucial things to learn as a tourist in a foreign country is the country's local language; with it, you can be more trusted and respected by locals.

In this chapter, I have compiled over 100 Japanese phrases that you can learn alongside their English translations; with them, you will feel more comfortable interacting with the locals.

Greetings and Basic Expressions

English	Japanese	Pronunciation
Hello	こんにちは	Konnichiwa
Good morning	おはようございます	Ohayou gozaimasu
Good evening	こんばんは	Konbanwa
Goodbye	さようなら	Sayounara

Good night	おやすみなさい	Oyasuminasai
Thank you	ありがとう	Arigatou
You're welcome	どういたしまして	Dou itashimashite
Excuse me/I'm sorry	すみません	Sumimasen
Yes	はい	Hai
No	いいえ	Iie
Essential Questions		
What is your name?	お名前は何ですか？	Onamae wa nan desu ka?
How are you?	お元気ですか？	Ogenki desu ka?
How much is it?	いくらですか？	Ikura desu ka?

What is this?	これは何ですか？	Kore wa nan desu ka?
Do you speak English?	英語を話せますか？	Eigo wo hanasemasu ka?
Where is the bathroom?	トイレはどこですか？	Toire wa doko desu ka?
Help me, please!	助けてください！	Tasukete kudasai!
What time is it?	何時ですか？	Nanji desu ka?
Where can I use Wi-Fi?	どこでWi-Fiを使えますか？	Doko de Wi-Fi wo tsukaemasu ka?
I speak a little Japanese	日本語を少し話します	Nihongo wo sukoshi hanashimasu
Dining		
Please show me	メニューを	Menyuu wo

the menu	見せてくだ さい	misete kudasai
I'll have this	これをくだ さい	Kore wo kudasai
It's delicious	美味しいで す	Oishii desu
Water, please	水をくださ い	Mizu wo kudasai
Check, please	お会計お願 いします	Okanjou onegaishimasu
I have an allergy	アレルギー があります	Alerugii ga arimasu
What do you recommend?	お勧めは何 ですか？	Osusume wa nan desu ka?
One beer, please	ビールを一 つください	Biiru wo hitotsu kudasai
Do you have salt	塩と胡椒は	Shio to koshou wa

and pepper?	ありますか？	arimasu ka?
Can I have this to go?	食べ物を持ち帰りできますか？	Tabemono wo mochikaeri dekimasu ka?
Directions and Transportation		
Where is the bus stop?	バス停はどこですか？	Basutei wa doko desu ka?
Does this train go to Tokyo?	この電車は東京に行きますか？	Kono densha wa Tokyo ni ikimasu ka?
Where do I change trains?	乗り換えはどこですか？	Norikae wa doko desu ka?
Where is the station?	駅はどこですか？	Eki wa doko desu ka?
Left	左	Hidari

Right	右	Migi
Straight ahead	まっすぐ	Massugu
I want to buy a ticket	切符を買いたいです	Kippu wo kaitai desu
Is that place far?	その場所は遠いですか？	Sono basho wa tooi desu ka?
How long does it take to the station?	駅までどのくらいかかりますか？	Eki made dono kurai kakarimasu ka?)
How much is this?	これはいくらですか？	Kore wa ikura desu ka?
Are there any recommended restaurants nearby?	近くにおすすめのレストランはありますか？	Chikaku ni osusume no resutoran wa arimasu ka?
What's the best way to get to the	空港への一番いい方法	Kuukou e no ichiban ii houhou

airport?	は何ですか？	wa nan desu ka?
Can you show me the map?	地図を見せてもらえますか？	Chizu wo misete moraemasuka?
Can you take a picture for me?	写真を撮ってもらえますか？	Shashin wo totte moraemasu ka?
What kind of meat is this?	これは何の肉ですか？	Kore wa nan no niku desu ka?
I am a vegetarian	私はベジタリアンです	Watashi wa bejitarian desu
Do you have an English menu?	英語のメニューはありますか？	Eigo no menyuu wa arimasu ka?
Please call a taxi for me	タクシーを呼んでください	Takushii wo yonde kudasai

44

I would like to make a reservation	予約をしたいのですが	Yoyaku wo shitai no desu ga
Please tell me about the tourist attractions in this area	この地域の観光名所を教えてください	Kono chiiki no kankou meisho wo oshiete kudasai
What time does this train/bus depart?	このアプリは便利ですか？	Kono apuri wa benri desu ka?
Where is the currency exchange?	交換所はどこですか？	Koukansho wa doko desu ka?
Can I use a credit card?	クレジットカードは使えますか？	Kurejitto kaado wa tsukaemasu ka?
Do you have an emergency contact?	緊急時の連絡先はありますか？	Kinkyuuji no renrakusaki wa arimasu ka?

Is this app useful?	この電車/バスは何時に出発しますか？	Kono densha/basu wa nanji ni shuppatsu shimasu ka?
Are you enjoying your stay in Japan?	日本での滞在を楽しんでいますか？	Nihon de no taizai wo tanoshinde imasu ka?
What should I buy for souvenirs?	お土産に何を買えばいいですか？	Omiyage ni nani wo kaeba ii desu ka?
What is the best sightseeing route?	ベストな観光ルートは何ですか？	Besuto na kankou ruuto wa nan desu ka?
Is the tap water drinkable?	水道水は飲めますか？	Suidousui wa nomemasu ka?
Where is the nearest bank?	最寄りの銀行はどこで	Moyori no ginkou wa doko desu ka?

	すか？	
Do you have something cheaper?	もっと安いものはありますか？	Motto yasui mono wa arimasu ka?
What are the business hours?	営業時間は何時から何時までですか？	Eigyou jikan wa nanji kara nanji made desu ka?
Is there free Wi-Fi?	この近くに郵便局はありますか？	Kono chikaku ni yuubinkyoku wa arimasu ka?
I want to buy some medicine	薬を買いたいです	Kusuri wo kaitai desu
I have a fever	熱があります	Netsu ga arimasu
Please call the police	無料のWi-Fiはありますか？	Muryou no Wi-Fi wa arimasu ka?

What time is check-out?	チェックアウトの時間は何時ですか？	Chekkuauto no jikan wa nanji desu ka?
Is there a hospital nearby?	病院は近くにありますか？	Byouin wa chikaku ni arimasu ka?
Is there a post office nearby?	警察を呼んでください	Keisatsu wo yonde kudasai
Could you say that again?	もう一度言ってもらえますか？	Mou ichido itte moraemasu ka?
Please avoid this ingredient due to allergies	アレルギーのため、この食材を避けてください	Arerugii no tame, kono shokuzai wo sakete kudasai
How do I use this?	これはどうやって使い	Kore wa douyatte tsukaimasu ka?

	ますか?	
Could you lower the volume?	音量を下げてもらえますか?	Onryou wo sagete moraemasu ka?
Do you have any food allergies?	苦手な食材がありますか?	Nigate na shokuzai ga arimasu ka?
I have allergies	アレルギーがあります	Arerugii ga arimasu
Do I need a reservation?	予約は必要ですか?	Yoyaku wa hitsuyou desu ka?
How do I adjust the air conditioning?	エアコンの調節はどうやってしますか?	Eakon no chousei wa douyatte shimasu ka?
Is this dish spicy?	この料理は辛いですか?	Kono ryouri wa karai desu ka?

I'd like a non-smoking seat, please	禁煙席をお願いします	Kinenseki wo onegaishimasu
Can you hold my luggage?	荷物を預かってもらえますか？	Nimotsu wo azukatte moraemasu ka?
Where is the emergency exit?	緊急出口はどこですか？	Kinkyuu deguchi wa doko desu ka?
Where is the lobby?	ロビーはどこですか？	Robii wa doko desu ka?
Which train should I take?	どの電車に乗ればいいですか？	Dono densha ni noreba ii desu ka?
Can I change rooms?	部屋を変えてもらえますか？	Heya wo kaete moraemasu ka?
What time is the	最終電車は何時ですか	Saishuu densha

last train?	?	wa nanji desu ka?
Excuse me, station staff	駅員さん、お願いします	Ekiin san, onegaishimasu
Do you have an air purifier?	空気清浄機はありますか？	Kuuki seijouki wa arimasu ka?
How do I get to this address?	このアドレスにどう行けばいいですか？	Kono adoresu ni dou ikeba ii desu ka?
Can you leave a message?	伝言を残してもらえますか？	Dengon wo nokoshite moraemasu ka?
I would like a quiet room	静かな部屋を希望します	Shizuka na heya wo kibou shimasu
Is breakfast included for	無料の朝食	Muryou no choushoku wa

51

free?	は含まれて いますか？	fukumarete imasu ka?
Can you tell me how to get to the hospital?	病院への行き方を教えてください。	Byouin e no ikikata wo oshiete kudasai
Do you have a vegetarian menu?	ベジタリアン向けのメニューはありますか？	
Can I borrow a Japanese plug adapter?	日本のプラグアダプターを貸してもらえますか？	Nihon no puragu adaputaa wo kashite moraemasu ka?
Can you book a taxi for me?	タクシーを予約してもらえますか？	Takushii wo yoyaku shite moraemasu ka?

Where do you recommend for jogging nearby?	この近くでジョギングするのにおすすめの場所は？	Kono chikaku de jogingu suru no ni osusume no basho wa?
Where is the ATM?	ATMはどこにありますか？	ATM wa doko ni arimasu ka?
Can you show me how to use the shower?	シャワーの使い方を教えてください。	Shawaa no tsukaikata wo oshiete kudasai
I'd like to know about the safety information for this area	この地域の安全情報を知りたいです。	Kono chiiki no anzen jouhou wo shiritai desu
What's the fastest way to get to the airport?	空港への最も速い交通手段は何で	Kuukou e no mottomo hayai koutsuu shudan

	すか？	wa nan desu ka?
Can you tell me how to take this medicine?	この薬の服用方法を教えてください。	Kono kusuri no fukuyou houhou wo oshiete kudasai.
Is there a discount for students?	学生割引はありますか？	Gakusei waribiki wa arimasu ka?
Where can I exchange foreign currency?	外貨両替の場所はどこですか？	Gaika ryougae no basho wa doko desu ka?
How many electrical outlets can I use?	最寄りのコンビニはどこですか？	Moyori no konbini wa doko desu ka?
Where can I download this app?	このアプリケーションはどこでダウンロードできますか	Kono apurikeeshon wa doko de daunroodo dekimasu ka?

	?	
Where is the nearest convenience store?	コンセントは何個使えますか？	Konsento wa nanko tsukaemasu ka?
Can I have the Wi-Fi password?	Wi-Fiのパスワードを教えてもらえますか？	Wi-Fi no pasuwaado wo oshiete moraemasu ka?
What should I do if I get lost?	道に迷ったらどうすればいいですか？	Michi ni mayottara dou sureba ii desu ka?
Do you offer laundry services?	ランドリーサービスはありますか？	Randorii saabisu wa arimasu ka?
Can you recommend a	良い本屋を	Yoi honya wo osusume

good bookstore?	おすすめできますか？	dekimasu ka?
How do I call international from Japan?	日本から国際電話をかける方法は？	Nihon kara kokusai denwa wo kakeru houhou wa?
How do I get a refund?	返金はどうすればいいですか？	Henkin wa dou sureba ii desu ka?
Do you know where I can buy a prepaid phone card?	プリペイドの電話カードをどこで買えますか？	Puripeido no denwa kaado wo doko de kaemasu ka?
Can I leave my luggage here before check-in?	チェックイン前に荷物をここに置いてもいいですか？	Chekkuin mae ni nimotsu wo koko ni oite mo ii desu ka?)

56

English	Japanese	Romaji
Can you help me order food online?	オンラインで食事を注文するのを手伝ってもらえますか？	Onrain de shokuji wo chuumon suru no wo tetsudatte moraemasu ka?
Where can I find a tourist information center?	観光情報センターはどこにありますか？	Kankou jouhou sentaa wa doko ni arimasu ka?
Can I rent a mobile phone?	携帯電話をレンタルできますか？	Keitai denwa wo rentaru dekimasu ka?
How much does it cost to use public transportation?	公共交通機関を利用するのにいくらかかりますか？	Koukyou koutsuukikan wo riyou suru no ni ikura kakarimasu ka?
Can you recommend a	地元のガイ	Jimoto no gaido wo osusume

local guide?	ドをおすすめできますか？	dekimasu ka?
Where can I buy a map of the city?	市内の地図をどこで買えますか？	Shinai no chizu wo doko de kaemasu ka?
Do I need to tip?	チップは必要ですか？	Chippu wa hitsuyou desu ka?
Is it safe to walk around here at night?	ここは夜歩いても安全ですか？	Koko wa yoru aruite mo anzen desu ka?
How can I connect to the local network?	地元のネットワークにどうやって接続しますか？	Jimoto no nettowaaku ni dou yatte setsuzoku shimasu ka?
What are the popular local dishes?	この地域の人気のある料理は何で	Kono chiiki no ninki no aru ryouri wa nan

	すか？	desu ka?
What is the emergency number?	緊急番号は何ですか？	Kinkyuu bangou wa nan desu ka?
How do I say this in Japanese?	これを日本語でどう言いますか？	Kore wo nihongo de dou iimasu ka?
What local beer do you recommend?	地ビールで何をおすすめしますか？	Ji biiru de nani wo osusume shimasu ka?
Can you recommend a quiet café?	静かなカフェをおすすめできますか？	Shizuka na kafe wo osusume dekimasu ka?
Is there a traditional Japanese inn nearby?	近くに日本式の宿泊施設はありますか？	Chikaku ni nihonshiki no shukuhaku shisetsu wa

		arimasu ka?
Where can I experience a tea ceremony?	どこで茶道を体験できますか？	Doko de sadou wo taiken dekimasu ka?
Can I drink the tap water?	水道の水は飲んでも大丈夫ですか？	Suidou no mizu wa nonde mo daijoubu desu ka?
How do I get to the nearest subway station?	最寄りの地下鉄の駅にはどう行けばいいですか？	Moyori no chikatetsu no eki ni wa dou ikeba ii desu ka?
What is the local specialty?	この地域の特産品は何ですか？	Kono chiiki no tokusanhin wa nan desu ka?
Where can I find vegetarian food?	ベジタリアン料理はどこで見つけ	Bejitarian ryouri wa doko de mitsukeraremasu

	られますか？	ka?
Is this area safe at night?	このエリアは夜に安全ですか？	Kono eria wa yoru ni anzen desu ka?
What time does the museum open?	博物館は何時に開きますか？	Hakubutsukan wa nanji ni hirakimasu ka?
What's the local cuisine like?	地元の料理はどんな感じですか？	Jimoto no ryouri wa donna kanji desu ka?
Can I have a receipt, please?	領収書をもらえますか？	Ryoushuusho wo moraemasu ka?
Can I buy a ticket online?	チケットをオンラインで買えますか？	Chiketto wo onrain de kaemasu ka?

Where is the nearest bicycle rental?	最寄りの自転車レンタルはどこですか？	Moyori no jitensha rentaru wa doko desu ka?
How do I use the washing machine?	洗濯機の使い方はどうですか？	Sentakuki no tsukaikata wa dou desu ka?
Can you call me a cab?	タクシーを呼んでいただけますか？	Takushii wo yonde itadakemasu ka?
Do you have Wi-Fi here?	ここにWi-Fiはありますか？	Koko ni Wi-Fi wa arimasu ka?
What is the check-in procedure?	チェックインの手続きは何ですか？	Chekkuin no tetsuzuki wa nan desu ka?
Is there a	近くに薬局	Chikaku ni

English	Japanese	Romaji
pharmacy nearby?	はあります か？	yakkyoku wa arimasu ka?
What should I do if I lose my passport?	パスポート を失くした 場合、どう すればいい ですか？	Pasupooto wo nakushita baai, dou sureba ii desu ka?
Can I enter with my shoes on?	靴を履いた まま入れま すか？	Kutsu wo haita mama hairemasu ka?
How far is the airport?	空港はどれ くらい遠い ですか？	Kuukou wa dore kurai tooi desu ka?
Can you suggest a day trip from here?	ここからの 日帰り旅行 を提案でき ますか？	Koko kara no higaeri ryokou wo teian dekimasu ka?

Tokyo

Tokyo offers a plethora of experiences that enthrall visitors, a city where the pulse of modernity beats in unison with the rhythm of centuries-old traditions. This expansive city, which seamlessly combines the old and the new, offers an adventure where something amazing is revealed around every corner. Tokyo is a city of contrasts that never ceases to amaze, from the calm beauty of its ancient temples and gardens to the neon-lit skyscrapers that define its skyline.

One of the busiest pedestrian crossings in the world, Shibuya Crossing, is where the sensory overload starts. You can see the well-organized chaos that perfectly captures Tokyo's dynamic lifestyle here. The neighborhood, a center of fashion and entertainment, is alive with activity day and night and provides a window into the youth culture that influences many of the popular trends in Japan. Close to this vibrant area is Harajuku, the center of kawaii (cute) culture, where the city's inventive energy is on display at every turn of the street and fashion knows no bounds.

Credit: <u>Acediscovery</u> via Wikimedia Commons

Even so, the verdant grounds of the Meiji Shrine or the placid waters of the Imperial Palace East Gardens offer some peace and quiet amid the city's unrelenting speed. These peaceful havens provide a break from the bustle of the city and a window into the nation's spiritual and royal past. Tokyo's exceptional ability to strike a balance between history and progress is demonstrated by the contrast between the calm, ancient sites and the city's fast-paced modern lifestyle.

Tokyo's world-class culinary scene is evidence of this. The city is a food lover's dream come true, with everything from fancy sushi bars where master chefs create edible works of art to the more casual izakayas and ramen cafes. With its wide selection of fresh fish and vegetables, the Tsukiji Outer Market offers a sense of the regional tastes that are essential to Japanese cooking. Tokyo dining is an exploration of flavors that showcase the creativity and diversity of the city, not just a means of subsistence.

Akihabara, the city's electric town, is a paradise for pop culture and technology aficionados, with every store stocked with the newest toys, anime, and manga. The rich tapestry of Japanese art and history is on display at the Edo-Tokyo Museum and the Mori Art Museum, which will pique the interest of art enthusiasts.

Tokyo offers a voyage that is as diverse as it is unforgettable, where tradition endures and the future is present. Tokyo is a city that is both intensely vibrant and incredibly charming, whether you're marveling at the state-of-the-art technology, learning about ancient customs, or enjoying delicious food.

What To Do and Don'ts

Tokyo is a fantastic city that has a lot to offer. You may respect the local way of life and people while taking full advantage of your stay by keeping some easy dos and don'ts in mind.

Do's:

1. **Do use public transport**: Tokyo's trains and buses are super efficient and a great way to get around.

2. **Do try local food**: From sushi to ramen, Tokyo's food scene is incredible. Don't miss out!

3. **Do respect local customs**: Bow when greeting people and say "thank you" in Japanese ("arigatou").

4. **Do take your shoes off**: When entering someone's home or certain traditional places, it's polite to remove your shoes.

5. **Do handle cash carefully**: Use both hands when giving or receiving money, especially at shops and temples.

6. **Do stay quiet on public transport**: It's considered polite to keep conversations low and not talk on your phone.

Don'ts:

1. **Don't tip:** Tipping is not a custom in Japan and can sometimes be seen as rude.

2. **Don't eat or drink while walking:** It's considered bad manners in many places. Find a spot to enjoy your snack.

3. **Don't ignore pedestrian lights**: Even if the road looks clear, wait for the green light to cross.

4. **Don't take photos without permission**: Especially when it comes to people or in private places. Look out for "No Photography" signs.

5. **Don't point:** Pointing at people or things is seen as impolite. Use an open hand gesture instead.

6. **Don't forget to queue**: Whether it's waiting for the train or buying tickets, orderly lines are a big part of Japanese culture.

6 Affordable Hotels in Tokyo

1. Makoto Guesthouse

Located in Tokyo's Adachi Ward, MAKOTO GUESTHOUSE -Enjoy your stay- offers air-conditioned accommodations just an 8-minute stroll from the Kameari Kochikame Statue. This guesthouse is known for its communal kitchen and lounge area, providing free WiFi across the premises. Guests can also enjoy evening entertainment and benefit from the concierge service available.

The guesthouse features rooms with shared bathrooms, equipped with a bidet and hairdryer. Certain rooms also include the added security of a safety deposit box. For convenience, each room comes with a refrigerator.

Nearby attractions include Higashiayase Park, the Kameari Katori Jinja Shrine, and the Ario Kameari Shopping Mall, making it a prime location for exploring local sights. Tokyo Haneda Airport is the closest airport, located 19 miles away from the guesthouse.

This spot has received positive reviews from couples, who have given it an 8.6 rating for stays for two, appreciating the location and amenities offered for a memorable trip.

Address: 121-0003 Tokyo-to, 足立区東和2-3-9, Japan

2. Almont Hotel Nippori (Hotel), Tokyo (Japan)

Perfectly situated in Tokyo's Arakawa Ward, Almont Hotel Nippori is just a brief five-minute stroll from Nippori South Park, within close proximity to Kyoouji Temple at 700 yards distance, and a seven-minute walk from the historic Site of Koda Rohan House. This three-star establishment boasts around-the-clock reception services and offers facilities for luggage storage. Notably, the Calligraphy Museum and the remnants of Tenno-ji

Temple Gojuno Tower are both just a seven-minute walk away.

Each room at the hotel is furnished with an electric kettle for your convenience. Guests will find all rooms air-conditioned, featuring a flat-screen TV for entertainment. Select rooms at Almont Hotel Nippori also offer picturesque mountain views. Comfort is a priority, with all accommodations provided with quality bed linen and towels.

For those keen to explore nearby attractions, Almont Hotel Nippori is close to the Asakura Museum of Sculpture, Shinkomutsumi Shopping Street, and Shikian, promising a culturally rich stay. Tokyo Haneda Airport, the nearest major airport, is located 15 miles away, making travel and transfers convenient.

This location has received high praise from couples, who have given it an 8.9 rating for a romantic or leisurely trip for two.

Address: 116-0014 Tokyo-to, Arakawa-ku Higashinippori 5-47-1, Japan

3. Muji Giza Hotel, Tokyo

Muji Hotel Ginza boasts a central location, placing you within walking distance of the city's vibrant energy. The hotel provides air-conditioned rooms, ideal for escaping the summer heat or enjoying a comfortable retreat after a day of exploration.

The hotel's guest rooms embody MUJI's philosophy of minimalist design. Each room features a desk and a TV, providing the essentials for work or relaxation. Beds are furnished with fresh linens and towels, ensuring a comfortable night's sleep.

The hotel's multilingual staff, fluent in English, Japanese, Korean, and Chinese, are always happy to assist you. Whether you need help navigating the city, recommending local attractions, or simply require general information, their friendly and knowledgeable team is at your service.

Address: 104-0061 Tokyo-to, 3-3-5 6F Ginza, Chuo-ku, Japan

4. Resol Poshtel Hotel Asakusa, Tokyo

Nestled in the vibrant Taito Ward of Tokyo, Resol Poshtel Tokyo Asakusa offers a prime location just a short stroll from the Drum Museum, mere steps from Kappabashi-dori Shopping Street, and close to Asakusa Public Hall. This capsule hotel, distinguished by its communal lounge, provides air-conditioned accommodations with complimentary WiFi access, all sharing modern communal bathrooms. It's conveniently situated a brief walk from Asakusa ROX Shopping Center and a short distance from the heart of the city, approximately 4.2 miles away.

Each capsule space is thoughtfully equipped with bed linens and towels for guest comfort.

Attractions nearby Resol Poshtel Tokyo Asakusa that guests frequently visit include Kinryu Park, Sogenji Temple, and Honpo-ji Temple, enriching their stay with cultural experiences. Tokyo Haneda

Airport is the closest major airport, located 15 miles from the hotel.

This location is especially favored by couples, who have given it a high rating of 9.3 for a getaway for two.

Address: 111-0035 Tokyo-to, Taito-ku Nishiasakusa 2-25-1, Japan

5. Hotel Yuni - Comfortable Stay Star - Club ID

Hotel Yuni's rooms offer a perfect haven for relaxation after a day of exploring the city. Whether you're traveling solo, as a couple, or with a small group, there's a room to accommodate your needs. The well-maintained space provides everything you need for a comfortable stay.

The hotel features a rooftop terrace, offering a fantastic spot to unwind and soak in the city vibe. This communal space is perfect for enjoying a morning cup of coffee with a view or relaxing in the evening after a day of sightseeing. Additional amenities like luggage storage and a welcoming lobby enhance the overall convenience of your stay.

Address: 162-0846 Tokyo-to, 市谷左内町22, Japan

6. KandO Hostel Ueno

KandO Hostel Ueno boasts an attractive location in Tokyo, placing you close to the action. Explore the city with ease and return to a comfortable haven after your adventures.

Escape the summer heat or relax after a day of sightseeing in your air-conditioned room. Each room provides a desk for working on your travel plans or catching up on emails.

Rooms at KandO Hostel Ueno offer comfortable beds with fresh linens and towels. The shared bathrooms are equipped with bidets, free toiletries, and hairdryers for your convenience.

Kando Hostel Ueno is surrounded by historical and cultural gems. Visit the serene Seigyo-ji Temple, explore the scenic Matsuba Park, or delve into the history of Tokaku-ji Temple. Numerous other temples, including Ryukoku-ji Temple, Hoon-ji Temple, and Rinko-ji Temple, are also within easy reach.

When it's time to depart, Tokyo Haneda Airport is conveniently located just 14 miles away. The hostel's central location also offers easy access to public transportation options so you can navigate the city with ease.

Address: *110-0015*   *Tokyo-to,*
台東区東上野６丁目８－７, *Japan*

5 Luxury Hotels in Tokyo

1. The Tokyo Station Hotel

Credit: PekePON via Wikimedia Commons

The Tokyo Station Hotel, ideally located just a 10-minute walk from Ginza, provides easy access to Akihabara and Asakusa. Situated within Tokyo Station, it offers convenient connections to airports, Shinkansen, JR lines, and subway, making it perfect

79

for exploring Japan. With a separate entrance ensuring privacy from station crowds, it maintains an exclusive atmosphere.

Credit: Asacyan via Wikimedia Commons

After a six-year reconstruction, the hotel combines vintage elegance with modern comforts. Its 150 suite rooms, starting from 40 m², offer stunning city views. Guests enjoy amenities like a fitness center, spa, and a variety of dining options, including sushi, French cuisine, and chic bars. With praise for its breakfast buffet and comfortable beds, The Tokyo

Station Hotel is an excellent choice for a luxurious staycation, offering smoking and non-smoking rooms.

Address: Chiyoda-ku Marunouchi 1-9-1, Tokyo, 100-0005

2. Four Seasons Hotel Tokyo at Otemachi

Perched atop a 39-story tower in central Tokyo, Four Seasons Hotel Tokyo at Otemachi offers panoramic city views, including landmarks like the Imperial Palace gardens and Tokyo Tower. With spacious rooms starting at 49 m² and renowned comfortable beds, it's perfect for families or groups. The hotel excels in hospitality, with attentive staff ready to assist and concierge services to plan your day. Indulge in gourmet dining options and unique experiences like whisky tastings. Unforgettable views and exceptional service await at this must-stay destination.

Address: Chiyoda-ku Otemachi 1-2-1, Tokyo, 100-0004

3. Andaz Toky

Andaz Tokyo, located in Toranomon's business hub near Kasumigaseki, offers a prime location close to the subway and Tokyo Tower. With 164 rooms atop a skyscraper, check-in at the 51st-floor Andaz Lounge sets a relaxed tone. The hotel showcases Japanese art throughout, adding to the cultural immersion.

Beyond its stylish design, Andaz Tokyo features a spa, fitness center, and indoor pool with city views. Rooms blend traditional Japanese elements with modern comforts and offer stunning vistas. Guests can enjoy complimentary snacks in Andaz Large rooms while taking in views of Tokyo Tower and Mount Fuji. For an elegant evening, the Rooftop Bar offers tea-infused cocktails and panoramic views of Tokyo Bay. With its blend of sophistication and convenience, Andaz Tokyo ensures a memorable stay.

Address: Minato-ku, Toranomon 1-23-4 , Tokyo, 105-0001

4. Tokyo Bay Shiomi Prince Hotel

Tokyo Bay Shiomi Prince Hotel offers a range of amenities including a restaurant, private parking, fitness center, and bar. This 4-star hotel provides a 24-hour front desk, luggage storage, and complimentary WiFi, with family rooms available.

Each guest room is equipped with a kettle and a private bathroom featuring a shower, slippers, and a hairdryer. Air conditioning, a safety deposit box, and a flat-screen TV are also provided for guests' comfort.

Guests can start their day with a buffet breakfast and later unwind in the sauna. Nearby attractions include Fukagawa Gatharia Shopping Mall,

Tatsuminomori Kaihin Park, and Susaki Stadium Monument. Tokyo Haneda International Airport is conveniently located 7.5 miles away from the hotel.

Address: 135-0052 Tokyo-to, Koto-ku Shiomi 2-8-16, Japan

5. Nohga Hotel Akihabara Tokyo

Conveniently situated in the heart of Tokyo, NOHGA HOTEL AKIHABARA TOKYO offers air-conditioned rooms, a restaurant, free WiFi, and a bar. This 4-star hotel provides a 24-hour front desk and luggage storage facilities. The entire property is smoke-free and is just a 2-minute walk from TKP Garden City Premium Akihabara.

All rooms at the hotel feature a flat-screen TV and a safety deposit box. Bed linen and towels are provided in each room at NOHGA HOTEL AKIHABARA TOKYO.

Nearby attractions include Akihabara Convention Hall, Yushima Seido, and Fujisoft Akiba Plaza.

Tokyo Haneda Airport is the closest airport, located 13 miles away from Nohga Hotel Akihabara Tokyo.

Address: 101-0021 Tokyo-to, Chiyoda-ku, Sotokanda 3-10-11, Japan

Children Playground in Tokyo

You're never too old to embrace a bit of silliness, and there's no better guide to goofy fun than a kid on vacation!

If you're traveling to Tokyo with children, here is the list of the top three playgrounds near popular family destinations like Skytree and Odaiba. With some careful planning, you can explore all the sights and still squeeze in some playground time.

Let's address the elephant in the room: Tokyo isn't exactly known for its impressive playgrounds. In fact, many are so small and unkempt that they're hardly deserving of the name. However, the parks I've selected here have all been thoroughly tested and approved by my daughter for their fun factor!

Finding time for playground breaks during vacation can be challenging, but it can also be the difference between a successful trip and a meltdown, especially in Japan where long lines are a common frustration for kids. So, without further ado, here are the top three playgrounds to add to your Tokyo itinerary.

1. Solamachi

Skytree is undoubtedly a fantastic choice for sightseeing in Tokyo. As the tallest man-made tower in Japan, it offers stunning views, including a glimpse of Mount Fuji on clear days. Even if you opt not to go to the top, simply seeing it up close is a memorable experience.

Moreover, it's worth noting that Solamachi, located at Skytree, houses some of Tokyo's rarest and most coveted shops, all conveniently situated in one place. Instead of enduring a three-hour wait for delicious popcorn at Omotesando, you can find it right here at Soramachi.

Soramachi also offers plenty of entertainment for kids, including an aquarium that's well worth the admission fee. However, if you're seeking a break from the crowds and want outdoor fun, there are two excellent playgrounds within walking distance from Skytree that are definitely worth exploring.

2. Wanpaku Tenkoku (Heaven)

A mere 10-minute stroll from Skytree leads to an exceptionally entertaining playground, Wanpaku Heaven, which remarkably doesn't charge admission—it's completely free!

Wanpaku Heaven boasts an enchanting old wooden fort complete with bridges, ladders, and a grand entrance gate (albeit sans drawbridge and moat). What truly sets this playground apart are the myriad extras it offers: unicycles, bikes, stilts, balls, carnival games, and even an open woodcraft workshop stocked with all the materials and tools imaginable. Some parents find themselves creating remarkable crafts alongside their children.

Location: 1 Chome-47-6 Oshiage, Sumida-ku, Tokyo-to 131-0045

Hours: 9am-6pm (5pm during winter)

Admission: Free

3. Oyokogawa Water Park

Just a short 10-minute walk west of Skytree lies one of Tokyo's intriguing river parks, nestled along a small man-made creek that winds through the city, adorned with tiny parks along its banks.

This riverside oasis offers a delightful respite from the bustling crowds, allowing visitors to unwind and stretch their legs. At the park's edge closest to Skytree stands a colossal ship-shaped building. Climbing to the roof rewards you with an exhilarating descent down a three-story pin-roller slide, albeit with a decidedly long and seat-numbing journey. Further along the path awaits another lengthy pin-roller slide, this time sans guardrails, adding an extra thrill to the experience.

Location: 1 Chome-47-6 Oshiage, Sumida-ku, Tokyo-to 131-0045

Hours: 9am-6pm

Admission: Free

Kyoto

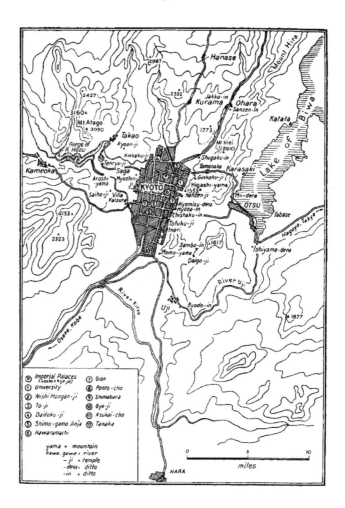

Credit: Viking Press, for the American edition, Public domain,

via Wikimedia Commons

Kyoto (京都, Kyōto) served as Japan's capital and the emperor's residence from 794 until 1868. It is one of the country's ten largest cities with 1.5 million inhabitants and a modern face.

Over the centuries, Kyoto was destroyed by many wars and fires, but due to its exceptional historic value, the city was dropped from the list of target cities for the atomic bomb and escaped destruction during World War II. Countless temples, shrines and other historically priceless structures survive in the city today.

Top Attractions in Kyoto

Kyoto Imperial Palace

The Kyoto Imperial Palace, once home to Japan's Imperial Family until 1868, now lies within the expansive Kyoto Imperial Park alongside the Sento Imperial Palace. Despite being reconstructed in 1855 following numerous relocations and fires, the current palace remains a historic marvel, enclosed by imposing walls and featuring gates, halls, and gardens. While visitors can freely explore the grounds, entry into the buildings is prohibited. Within the park, other attractions include the Kaninnomiya Mansion and a small branch shrine of Miyajima's Itsukushima Shrine. Spanning 1300 meters by 700 meters, the park offers ample recreational space with gravel paths, lawns, and tree groves, highlighted by the stunning weeping cherry trees beside Konoe Pond, typically in bloom from late March to mid-April.

Kyoto Railway Museum

Opened in 2016 by JR West on the former site of the Umekoji Train and Locomotive Museum, the Kyoto Railway Museum offers a fascinating exploration of Japan's railway history. Situated a short walk west of Kyoto Station, this museum spans three floors and 30,000 square meters, displaying over 50 retired trains ranging from steam locomotives to modern shinkansen. Visitors can observe the inner workings of a retired freight locomotive, explore interactive exhibitions, and enjoy scenic views of passing trains from the restaurant and observation deck on the second floor.

Adjacent to the main building, a roundhouse dating back to 1914 houses Japan's largest collection of well-preserved steam locomotives. Visitors can witness real-time train maintenance and even take a one-kilometer journey on a steam locomotive-powered train for a nominal fee. At the museum's exit stands the picturesque Nijo Station Building, a relic of Japan's railway history dating back to 1904, offering a nostalgic glimpse into the country's bygone era of railway construction.

Sento Imperial Palace

Situated across from the Kyoto Imperial Palace within Kyoto Imperial Park, the Sento Imperial

Palace (Sentō Gosho) has a rich history dating back to its establishment in 1630 as the retirement residence of Emperor Gomizuno. Over the years, it has served as the retirement abode for successive emperors.

In 1854, the original palace structures succumbed to fire and were not reconstructed. Instead, Omiya Palace was built on the Sento grounds in 1867, now serving as the lodging for the current prince and princess during their visits to Kyoto.

Access to the Sento Imperial Palace is available exclusively through free tours organized by the Imperial Household Agency. These tours offer an opportunity to explore the palace garden, including the North Pond and South Pond areas, renowned for their picturesque strolling gardens. Although conducted solely in Japanese, audio guides in various foreign languages are provided. While entry into the palace buildings is restricted, some structures such as the Seikatei teahouse are accessible, offering visitors glimpses into imperial architecture and aesthetics.

Pontocho

Pontocho (Pontochō) stands out as one of Kyoto's most captivating dining districts, characterized by its narrow alley stretching from Shijo-dori to Sanjo-dori, just a block west of the Kamogawa River. Lined with eateries on both sides, Pontocho offers a diverse culinary experience, ranging from affordable yakitori to traditional and contemporary Kyoto cuisine, as well as international fare and exclusive dining spots requiring connections and deep pockets.

While the operating hours and days off vary among the establishments along Pontocho, most are typically open from around 5:00 PM to 11:00 PM, with some also serving lunch. Many restaurants provide English menus for the convenience of international visitors. Along the eastern side of the alley, numerous dining spots offer views of the Kamogawa River, with some constructing temporary platforms over the water from May to September. Known as kawayuka, this unique dining experience allows patrons to enjoy traditional Kyoto dishes amidst the refreshing breeze and lively summer ambiance. Reservations for kawayuka are advisable, particularly on Fridays and Saturdays.

Okinawa

Okinawa, a gem in Japan, is celebrated for its untouched beaches, deep-rooted cultural traditions, and lively underwater world, offering a rich array of attractions for every type of traveler. Shurijo Castle, nestled in Naha City, is a UNESCO World Heritage Site that once served as the central palace of the Ryukyu Kingdom. Today, it stands as a testament to Okinawa's historical depth and endurance. Guests are invited to wander through the castle's majestic chambers, admire its detailed designs, and stroll its verdant grounds, all while uncovering the intriguing history of Okinawa.

Another highlight is the Churaumi Aquarium, located within Ocean Expo Park in Motobu. This premier aquarium is home to a vast variety of sea creatures, including whale sharks, manta rays, and vibrant coral reefs. Its centerpiece, the colossal Kuroshio Tank, is among the biggest of its kind globally, offering a captivating view into the rich marine ecosystem of Okinawa.

Nature lovers will find their paradise at the Okinawa Churaumi Tropical Botanical Garden in the island's northern reaches. This botanical haven is filled with an impressive assortment of tropical flora, showcasing the unique plant life of Okinawa and other tropical regions. Guests can meander through the verdant landscapes, admire rare and exotic plants, and take in stunning views of the natural surroundings.

Moreover, Kabira Bay on Ishigaki Island is a quintessential stop for those drawn to the ocean's allure. Famous for its translucent waters and breathtaking vistas, Kabira Bay is a sanctuary for snorkeling, diving, and unwinding on its pristine beaches. Boat tours offer a unique opportunity to discover the bay's secluded nooks, coral gardens, and abundant marine inhabitants, making it a prime location for admirers of the natural world.

1. Shurijo Castle

Shuri Castle, a World Heritage site by UNESCO, once the hub of Ryukyu Kingdom's governance, now allows visitors to journey through Okinawa's noble history. Witness the castle's vibrant royal chambers, expansive courtyards, and intricate design, all reconstructed post-World War II.

Address: 1 Chome-2 Shurikinjocho, Naha, Okinawa 903-0815, Japan

2. Churaumi Aquarium

Famous for housing the world's most substantial acrylic tank, this aquarium presents the grand whale shark among a breathtaking assortment of marine species. Experience the captivating feeding shows and gain insight into Okinawa's critical role in marine conservation.

Address: 424 Ishikawa, Motobu, Kunigami District, Okinawa 905-0206, Japan

3. Kabira Bay

A paradise of crystal-clear waters and scenic beauty, Kabira Bay is unparalleled for water activities like snorkeling and diving, or for simply soaking up the sun on its soft, sandy shores. The bay offers boat tours for visitors to explore its secluded areas, coral ecosystems, and vibrant aquatic life, promising an unforgettable experience for all who venture there.

Address: Kabira, Ishigaki, Okinawa 907-0453, Japan

Cultural Insights

Japanese Cuisine

Japanese cuisine, known as "washoku," offers an exquisite blend of taste, tradition, and artistic presentation, deeply rooted in seasonal changes and regional diversity. It's a culinary experience that embodies the essence of Japanese aesthetics and philosophy, with an emphasis on fresh, seasonal ingredients, minimalistic preparation, and harmonious flavors. Japanese cuisine is recognized globally for its health benefits, intricate balance of flavors, and unique dining rituals. From sushi to ramen, each dish tells a story of cultural heritage and culinary innovation.

When visiting Japan, tourists are encouraged to immerse themselves in the local food culture by trying a variety of traditional dishes. Here are 10 essential Japanese dishes that provide a taste of the country's rich culinary landscape:

1. **Sushi and Sashimi**: Sushi, vinegared rice accompanied by seafood or vegetables, and Sashimi, thinly sliced raw fish, are iconic Japanese dishes. They showcase the freshness and quality of local seafood, served with soy sauce, wasabi, and pickled ginger.

2. **Ramen**: A popular noodle soup dish that consists of Chinese-style wheat noodles served in a meat or fish-based broth, often flavored with soy sauce or miso, with toppings such as sliced pork, nori (seaweed), menma (bamboo shoots), and green onions.

3. **Tempura**: This is a dish of seafood or vegetables that have been lightly battered and deep-fried, known for its delicate, crispy texture. Tempura is often served with a tentsuyu dip (a mix of soy sauce, mirin, and dashi).

4. **Takoyaki**: A street food favorite, these are ball-shaped snacks made of a wheat flour-based batter and cooked with minced or diced octopus, tempura

scraps, pickled ginger, and green onion, typically topped with takoyaki sauce, mayonnaise, and bonito flakes.

5. **Okonomiyaki**: Often referred to as Japanese savory pancakes, okonomiyaki are made with a batter mixed with cabbage and various ingredients such as seafood, meat, and vegetables, grilled and usually topped with okonomiyaki sauce, mayonnaise, green onions, and bonito flakes.

6. **Tonkatsu**: A breaded and deep-fried pork cutlet, served sliced with shredded cabbage, miso soup, rice, and a thick, sweet sauce called tonkatsu sauce. Variations include katsu curry (tonkatsu served with

curry) and katsudon (tonkatsu served over rice with egg).

7. **Yakitori**: Skewered and grilled chicken, yakitori is a popular izakaya (Japanese pub) dish. It can include various parts of the chicken, from breast to heart, seasoned primarily with salt or tare sauce (a sweet soy sauce-based glaze).

8. **Soba and Udon:** Both are traditional Japanese noodles but differ in ingredients and texture. Soba is made from buckwheat flour, offering a nutty flavor, served either chilled with a dipping sauce or in a hot broth. Udon is thicker, wheat-based noodles, known for their chewy texture, served hot in a savory dashi-based broth.

9. **Kaiseki Ryori:** A traditional multi-course Japanese dinner that emphasizes seasonal ingredients, presentation, and balance in taste. Kaiseki meals are an art form, reflecting the season and the chef's technique through meticulously prepared dishes.

10. **Matcha and Wagashi**: No culinary exploration of Japan is complete without experiencing the traditional tea ceremony, which features matcha (powdered green tea) and wagashi (Japanese sweets). Wagashi, made from ingredients like mochi, anko (red bean paste), and fruits, perfectly complements the bitter taste of matcha.

Japanese Festivals You've Never Heard Of

Japanese festivals (matsuri) are an integral part of the country's culture, reflecting its rich history, spirituality, and community spirit. While some festivals like Tokyo's Sanja Matsuri or Kyoto's Gion Matsuri are famous worldwide, there are numerous lesser-known festivals across Japan that offer unique experiences and insights into local customs. Here are several intriguing Japanese festivals that you might not have heard of, but are certainly worth the detour:

1. **Nebuta Matsuri (Aomori):** Held annually from August 2 to 7 in Aomori, the Nebuta Matsuri features gigantic, illuminated floats depicting

110

warrior figures and mythical beings. These vibrant, handcrafted floats are paraded through the streets at night, accompanied by traditional music, dancers, and drummers, creating a spectacle of light and sound. It's a festival that showcases the artistry and craftsmanship of the region.

2. **Naked Man Festival (Hadaka Matsuri) (Okayama)**: The Hadaka Matsuri, or Naked Man Festival, takes place in Saidaiji, Okayama, on the third Saturday of February. Participants, mostly men wearing only a loincloth (fundoshi), battle in the cold to grab a pair of sacred sticks thrown by a priest into the crowd. It's a test of endurance and faith, believed to bring good fortune and purification.

3. **Yuki Matsuri (Sapporo Snow Festival) (Hokkaido):** Although relatively well-known, the Sapporo Snow Festival in early February transforms Hokkaido's capital into a winter wonderland of snow and ice sculptures. Artists from around the world create massive, intricate sculptures that illuminate the night, alongside ice bars, concerts, and snow slides, making it a magical experience for all ages.

4. **Kanamara Matsuri (Kawasaki):** The Kanamara Matsuri, or "Festival of the Steel Phallus," held annually on the first Sunday of April at the Kanayama Shrine in Kawasaki, celebrates fertility, marriage, and healthy childbirth. It's known for its

phallic imagery, including sculptures, candies, and carved vegetables, paraded around in a lively, joyous atmosphere that welcomes everyone.

5. **Onbashira Festival (Nagano):** Occurring every six years (next in 2022), the Onbashira Festival involves the symbolic renewal of the Suwa Taisha Shrine. The highlight is the "kiotoshi" ritual, where massive logs are ridden down steep slopes by participants, demonstrating bravery and invoking the gods' blessings. It's a dramatic spectacle of human endurance and spiritual devotion.

6. **Hiwatari Matsuri (Fire Walking Festival) (Mount Takao, Tokyo):** The Fire Walking Festival, held annually in March at the foot of

113

Mount Takao, sees Yamabushi (mountain ascetic hermits) walk over smoldering coals after performing purification rituals. Spectators can also participate, walking barefoot over the cooled ashes for purification and to ward off evil spirits.

7. **Hounen Matsuri (Komaki):** Celebrated every March 15th in Komaki, north of Nagoya, the Hounen Matsuri is another fertility festival, famous for its 2.5-meter-long wooden phallus, which is carried from a shrine to another in a lively procession. It's a celebration of prosperity, fertility, and the arrival of spring, attracting thousands of participants and spectators.

Practical Information

Safety Tips and Emergency Information

Traveling to Japan is an exciting adventure, offering a blend of ancient traditions, cutting-edge technology, breathtaking landscapes, and vibrant city life. Japan is renowned for its safety, cleanliness, and the politeness of its people. However, like any travel destination, it's crucial to be prepared and aware of safety tips and emergency information to ensure a smooth and enjoyable experience.

General Safety Tips

1. **Stay Informed**: Before and during your trip, keep an eye on local news and weather forecasts.

Japan is prone to natural disasters like earthquakes, typhoons, and heavy rains that can lead to flooding and landslides.

2. **Emergency Alerts:** Install apps like "Safety Tips," developed by the Japan Tourism Agency, which provides disaster alerts and helpful information in English.

3. **Respect Local Customs**: Japanese society values respect and politeness. Understanding and adhering to local customs, such as removing shoes before entering homes and some restaurants, will help avoid unintentional disrespect.

4. **Travel Insurance:** Ensure you have comprehensive travel insurance that covers medical expenses, including those that may arise from natural disasters or unexpected events.

5. **Keep Valuables Safe:** Although Japan has a low crime rate, always practice caution with your belongings, especially in crowded places like train stations and tourist spots.

Natural Disasters Preparedness

1. **Earthquakes**: Japan is located in an earthquake-prone zone. Familiarize yourself with safety measures, such as Drop, Cover, and Hold On during shaking. Learn how to turn off gas and water lines if you're staying in an Airbnb or rental.

2. **Typhoons:** Typhoon season typically runs from June to October. Secure loose items if you're staying near coastal areas, and follow evacuation orders if issued.

3. **Tsunamis**: Coastal areas may be at risk of tsunamis following an earthquake. Pay attention to warnings and know the evacuation routes to higher ground or designated shelters.

Health and Medical Emergencies

1. **Medical Facilities:** Japan offers high-quality medical care. However, not all staff may speak English fluently. It's beneficial to know the Japanese terms for basic ailments and to have a translation app handy.

2. **Pharmacies**: Medications that are over-the-counter in your home country may require a prescription in Japan. Carry a doctor's note for any

prescription medicines, and be aware of any banned substances.

3. **Emergency Numbers**: Know the key emergency numbers in Japan—110 for police and 119 for fire and ambulance services. Also, keep the contact information of your embassy or consulate.

In Case of an Emergency

1. **Communication:** In addition to emergency apps, consider renting a pocket Wi-Fi or purchasing a local SIM card to ensure you can access help and information when needed.

2. **Local Support:** Look for information centers or police boxes (koban) in case you need directions, lose something, or need assistance. Staff at hotels

and major train stations are also typically helpful in emergencies.

3. **Emergency Evacuation Sites**: Major cities and towns in Japan have designated evacuation sites in case of natural disasters. Familiarize yourself with the nearest site to your accommodation.

4. **Stay Calm and Follow Instructions**: In any emergency, stay calm and follow the instructions given by local authorities or your emergency app alerts.

Shopping in Japan

Shopping in Japan is an unparalleled experience that combines traditional markets, cutting-edge electronics stores, and everything in between. The country's retail spaces range from historic streets filled with centuries-old craftsmanship to futuristic malls showcasing the latest in fashion and technology.

Whether you're looking for unique souvenirs, high-end fashion, or the latest gadgets, Japan offers a shopping experience that caters to every interest and budget. Here is a comprehensive guide to shopping in Japan, including 9 to 11 places where tourists can indulge in retail therapy, complete with addresses for your convenience.

1. Ginza, Tokyo

Address: Ginza, Chuo, Tokyo

Ginza is Tokyo's premier shopping district, known for its upscale boutiques, department stores, and gourmet dining options. Here, you'll find flagship stores of luxury brands, the iconic Wako department store with its famous clock tower, and the multi-story Uniqlo Ginza, one of the largest Uniqlo stores in the world.

2. Akihabara, Tokyo

Address: Akihabara, Taito, Tokyo

A haven for electronics enthusiasts and anime fans, Akihabara is packed with stores offering the latest gadgets, video games, manga, and anime merchandise. Don't miss the Akihabara Electric Town for electronic goods and the Mandarake Complex for pre-owned manga and anime items.

3. Shibuya, Tokyo

Address: Shibuya, Tokyo

Shibuya is the epitome of Tokyo's youthful fashion scene, with Shibuya Crossing at its heart. Highlights include Shibuya 109, a landmark with multiple floors of fashion boutiques catering to young women, and the recently opened Shibuya Scramble Square for high-end shopping and dining.

4. Harajuku, Tokyo

Address: Harajuku, Shibuya, Tokyo

Harajuku is famous for its street fashion, vintage clothing stores, and quirky boutiques. Takeshita Street is a must-visit for trendy, affordable fashion, while Omotesando offers a more upscale shopping experience with designer boutiques and chic cafes.

5. Dotonbori, Osaka

Address: Dotonbori, Chuo-ku, Osaka

Dotonbori is Osaka's bustling entertainment and shopping district, known for its extravagant neon lights and giant shop signs. It's a great place to shop for souvenirs, try local street food, and experience the vibrant Kansai culture.

6. Namba Parks, Osaka

Address: 2 Chome-10-70 Nambanaka, Naniwa Ward, Osaka

Namba Parks is an innovative shopping and entertainment complex with a strikingly designed rooftop garden. It offers a wide range of shops, from fashion to lifestyle goods, alongside cinemas and restaurants with a view.

7. Shinsaibashi, Osaka

Address: Shinsaibashi, Chuo-ku, Osaka

Shinsaibashi is Osaka's largest shopping area, featuring a long-covered shopping arcade that stretches for several blocks. Here, you can find international brands, Japanese boutiques, and traditional goods, making it a perfect spot for all types of shoppers.

8. Teramachi and Shinkyogoku Shopping Arcades, Kyoto

Address: Nakagyo Ward, Kyoto

In the heart of Kyoto, the Teramachi and Shinkyogoku Shopping Arcades are two parallel streets offering a mix of traditional and modern shopping experiences. These arcades are home to a variety of shops selling souvenirs, crafts, clothing, and more, as well as cafes and restaurants serving Kyoto cuisine.

9. Canal City Hakata, Fukuoka

Address: 1 Chome-2 Sumiyoshi, Hakata Ward, Fukuoka

Canal City Hakata is a large shopping and entertainment complex in Fukuoka, dubbed a "city within the city." Its design incorporates water canals and fountains, and it houses over 250 shops, restaurants, a theater, and a cinema.

10. Kokusai Dori, Okinawa

Address: Kokusai Dori, Naha, Okinawa

Kokusai Dori, or "International Road," is the main street in Naha, Okinawa, known for its lively atmosphere, souvenir shops, and restaurants serving Okinawan cuisine. It's an excellent place to buy traditional Okinawan crafts, such as Ryukyu glassware and Shisa (lion-dog) statues.

11. Omicho Market, Kanazawa

Address: 50 Kamiomicho, Kanazawa, Ishikawa

Often referred to as "Kanazawa's Kitchen," Omicho Market has been the city's largest fresh food market since the Edo period. It's a fantastic place to explore the local cuisine, with numerous stalls selling seafood, fruits, vegetables, and sweets, as well as restaurants where you can enjoy fresh sushi and seafood bowls. This market offers an authentic glimpse into the culinary culture of the Hokuriku region and is a must-visit for food enthusiasts.

Off the Beaten Path

Japan reveals a side of the country that many travelers overlook, one where tranquil landscapes, sacred traditions, and heart-pounding activities await.

Discovering Japan's Rural Charm

Japan's countryside offers a serene escape into regions where time seems to slow down, and nature takes center stage. The rural landscapes of Japan are a tapestry of verdant rice fields, traditional thatched-roof houses, and small villages that celebrate the changing seasons with festivals and art.

- **Shirakawa-go and Gokayama**: Nestled in the mountainous region of central Japan, these villages are renowned for their traditional gassho-zukuri farmhouses, some of which are over 250 years old. The architectural style, designed to withstand heavy snowfall, creates a picturesque scene, especially in winter when the area is blanketed in snow.

- **Kiso Valley**: Home to the historic Nakasendo trail, Kiso Valley offers a glimpse into the Edo period with its well-preserved post towns of Magome and Tsumago. Hiking between these towns is a beautiful way to experience Japan's natural beauty and historical architecture.

Pilgrimages and Sacred Sites

Japan's rich spiritual heritage is reflected in its numerous pilgrimages and sacred sites, many of which are nestled in remote, tranquil locations that offer a profound sense of peace and reflection.

- **Kumano Kodo**: An ancient network of pilgrimage routes in the Kii Mountains, the Kumano Kodo is a UNESCO World Heritage site that has been traveled for over a thousand years. Pilgrims traverse forested paths to reach three grand shrines, Kumano Hongu Taisha, Kumano Nachi Taisha, and Kumano Hayatama Taisha, a journey that is as spiritual as it is physical.

- **Mount Koya (Koyasan):** The center of Shingon Buddhism, Koyasan is a sacred mountain retreat filled with temples, shrines, and the Okunoin Cemetery. Staying overnight in a temple lodging (shukubo) and participating in morning prayers offers a unique insight into monastic life.

Adventure Sports and Where to Find Them

For those seeking adrenaline, Japan's varied landscape provides a playground for numerous outdoor activities, from snow sports in the north to water sports in the south.

- **Niseko:** Located on the northern island of Hokkaido, Niseko is famed for its powder snow, making it a paradise for skiers and snowboarders from around the world. The area also offers opportunities for snowmobiling, snowshoeing, and onsen hopping after a long day on the slopes.

- **Yakushima**: An island off the southern coast of Kyushu, Yakushima is a haven for hikers and nature lovers. The island's ancient cedar forests, home to trees that are thousands of years old, provide a mystical backdrop for trekking. The rugged terrain, waterfalls, and wildlife make it an unforgettable destination for adventurers.

- **Okinawa**: The tropical islands of Okinawa are ideal for water sports enthusiasts. With its crystal-clear waters, coral reefs, and abundant marine life, Okinawa offers some of the best diving and snorkeling in Japan. Kayaking, surfing, and paddleboarding are also popular activities that allow visitors to explore the islands' natural beauty.

Conclusion

Traveling to Japan is like traveling to another universe, one in which the past and present live side by side and where every turn reveals a mosaic of enduring customs, breathtaking scenery, and cutting-edge invention.

Japan invites visitors to fully immerse themselves in experiences that go beyond the ordinary because of its unmatched combination of natural beauty and cultural legacy. Every location in this amazing nation, from the calm grandeur of Mount Fuji to the hallowed serenity of its temples and shrines, has a distinct history to tell, providing an insight into a long-standing tale that is still relevant today.

Allow the beauty and exploration of Japan to permeate your travels as you get ready to go off on this adventure.

Seize the chance to discover, interact, and learn from the people and places you encounter as well as from the locations you visit.

43043525R00076